moxie

These quotations were gathered lovingly but unscientifically over several years and/or were contributed by many friends or acquaintances. Some arrived—and survived in our files—on scraps of paper and may therefore be imperfectly worded or attributed. To the authors, contributors and original sources, our thanks, and where appropriate, our apologies.—The Editors

CREDITS

Compiled by Kobi Yamada
Designed by Steve Potter

ISBN: 978-1-888387-66-7

3rd Printing. 5K 03 09   Printed in China

Think of the world you carry inside you.

RAINER   MARIA   RILKE

All of us are
crazy good
in one way
or another.

YIDDISH SAYING

You are everything that is,

your thoughts, your life,

your dreams come true.

You are everything you choose to be.

You are as unlimited

as the endless universe.

SHAD HELMSTETTER

The best day of your life is the one on which you decide your life is your own. No apologies or excuses. No one to lean on, rely on or blame. The gift of life is yours; it is an amazing journey; and you alone are responsible for the quality of it.

DAN ZADRA

Give the historians
something to write about.

PROPERTIUS

Be afraid
of nothing—
you have within you
all wisdom,
all power,
all strength,
all understanding.

EILEEN CADDY

THERE IS MORE HERE
THAN MEETS THE EYE.

LADY MURASAKI

...FULL OF THE STRENGTH OF FIVE.

SIR JOHN BETJEMAN

Believe

that you have it,

and you have it.

LATIN PROVERB

YOUR SPARK
CAN BECOME
A FLAME AND
CHANGE
EVERYTHING.

E. D. NIXON

We all have the extraordinary coded within us, waiting to be released.

JEAN HOUSTON

Realize how good you really are.

OG MANDINO

You already possess

everything necessary

to become great.

PROVERB

So many worlds,

so much to do,

so little done,

such things to be.

ALFRED, LORD TENNYSON

IT IS NOT GIVEN US
TO LIVE LIVES
OF UNDISRUPTED CALM, BOREDOM,
AND MEDIOCRITY.
IT IS GIVEN US
TO BE EDGE-DWELLERS.

JAY DEACON

I am here to live out loud.

ÉMILE ZOLA

We are the
music-makers,
And we are
the dreamers
of dreams.
...Yet we are the
movers and
shakers
Of the world
for ever,
it seems.

ARTHUR O'SHAUGHNESSY

We are all boundless creatures.

KOBI YAMADA

The molecules of your body are the same molecules that make up the nebulae, that burn inside the stars themselves. We are starstuff.

D.C. FONTANA

What you want,
baby I got it.

ARETHA FRANKLIN

I WANT TO BE EVERYBODY, AND I WANT TO BE EVERYTHING. ONE LIFE IS NOT ENOUGH.

VLADIMIR SOKOLOFF

I AM NOT A MAN,
I AM DYNAMITE.

FRIEDRICH NIETZSCHE

If it's me
against 48,
I feel sorry for
the 48.

MARGARET THATCHER

I am not bound
to win, but I
am bound to
be true. I am
not bound to
succeed, but I
am bound to live
up to what light
I might have.

ABRAHAM LINCOLN

I am larger,
better than
I thought,
I did not know
I held so much
goodness.

WALT WHITMAN

We have the power, knowledge and equipment to build a world beyond our wonder. Only loss of nerve can defeat us. That is all. A loss of nerve.

JAMES DILLET FREEMAN

Energy rightly
applied
and directed
will accomplish
anything.

NELLIE BLY

I believe that when you realize who you really are, you understand that nothing can stop you from becoming that person.

CHRISTINE LINCOLN

I WILL DARE
TO JUST DO WHAT
I DO. BE JUST
WHAT I AM.
AND DANCE WHENEVER
I WANT TO.

BEVERLY WILLIAMS

STAND IN YOUR OWN SPACE AND
KNOW YOU ARE THERE.

ANSON HEIGEL

I will not die an unlived life.
I will not live in fear of
falling or catching fire.
I choose to inhabit my days,
to allow my living to open
me, to make me less afraid,
more accessible, to loosen
my heart until it becomes
a wing, a torch, a promise.

DAWNA MARKOVA

I AM NOT AFRAID…
I WAS BORN TO DO THIS.

JOAN OF ARC

BELIEVE ME! THE SECRET

OF REAPING THE GREAT-

EST FRUITFULNESS AND

THE GREATEST ENJOY-

MENT FROM LIFE IS TO LIVE

DANGEROUSLY!

FRIEDRICH NIETZSCHE

Do not
    fear death
so much,
    but rather the
inadequate life.

BERTOLT BRECHT

Do we dare

be ourselves?

That is

the question

that counts.

PABLO CASALS

Born originals,
how comes it
to pass that
we die copies?

E D W A R D   Y O U N G

To be nobody-but-your-self in a world which is doing its best, night and day to make you somebody else means to fight the hardest battle which any human being can fight; and never stop fighting.

E.E. CUMMINGS

If one is
forever
cautious,
can one
remain a
human
being?

ALEKSANDR SOLZHENITSYN

YOU ARE YOU.
THERE IS ONLY
ONE YOU.
AND YOU ARE IMPORTANT.
AND DON'T YOU DARE
CHANGE
JUST BECAUSE YOU'RE
OUTNUMBERED!

CHARLES SWINDOLL

Fortune favors the bold.

VIRGIL

Give me a
place to stand
and I will move
the world.

ARCHIMEDES

THEY CAN'T CENSOR THE
GLEAM IN MY EYE.

CHARLES LAUGHTON

Do you want
to be a power
in the world?
Then be
yourself.

RALPH WALDO TRINE

Our deepest fear is not that we are inadequate. Our deepest fear is that we are powerful beyond measure. It is our light, not our darkness, that frightens us most. We ask ourselves, who am I to be brilliant, gorgeous, talented and fabulous? Actually who are you not to be? You are a child of the universe. You were born to manifest the glory of the universe that is within us. It's not just in some of us; it's in everyone.

MARIANNE WILLIAMSON

Like
the moon,
come out
from behind
the clouds.
Shine!

BUDDHA

Not all horses

were born equal.

A few were

born to win.

UNKNOWN

HAVE THE COURAGE OF YOUR DESIRE.

GEORGE R. GISSING

When you
cannot make
up your mind
which of two
evenly balanced
courses of
action, choose
the bolder.

GENERAL W.J. SLIM

YOU CAN'T LEAD A

CAVALRY CHARGE IF

YOU THINK YOU LOOK

FUNNY ON A HORSE.

JOHN PEERS

MASQUERADING
AS A NORMAL PERSON
DAY AFTER
DAY IS
EXHAUSTING.

U N K N O W N

Don't go
with the flow.
You are
the flow.

SUGI TANAKA

At times
it is necessary
to go over the top.
How else can we
get to the
other side?

KOBI YAMADA

COME, GIVE US A TASTE OF YOUR QUALITY.

WILLIAM SHAKESPEARE

Each of us has a spark of life inside us, and our highest endeavor ought to be to set off that spark in one another.

KENNY AUSUBEL

The only thing
that keeps
one going
is energy.
And what
is energy
but liking life?

LOUIS AUCHINCLOSS

Nothing can

dim the light

which shines

from within.

MAYA ANGELOU

A POSSIBILITY WAS BORN
THE DAY YOU WERE BORN
AND IT WILL LIVE AS
LONG AS YOU LIVE.

MARCUS SOLERO